PURPOSE REVIVAL

LEARNING HOW TO DO THE GREATER THINGS

JOHN W. STANKO

urbanpress

Purpose Revival
by John W. Stanko
Copyright ©2022 John W. Stanko

ISBN 978-1-63360-202-1

For Worldwide Distribution   Printed in the U.S.A.

Urban Press
P.O. Box 8881
Pittsburgh, PA 15221-0881
412.646.2780
www.urbanpress.us

INTRODUCTION

I've been teaching people how to find their purpose since 1991, all the while producing resources—seminars, books, podcasts, blog posts—so they could ask the right questions and get the best answers where purpose is concerned. Some people warned me early on that I would eventually have to expand my repertoire of messages at some point, since the purpose message would run its course and I would at that point find myself irrelevant.

Yet here I am thirty years later, and the purpose message is more relevant than ever. I'm going strong with two companies, dozens of books, and thousands of people touched through my posts written and presentations made about purpose. And lately when I teach about purpose, I've found that some people depart my presence having had a personal revival of sorts—whether it was one on one or a group seminar. The purpose message is so powerful and the need so urgent that God is still transforming people as they accept the message and find their purpose, just like He did when I first started—and maybe more so.

Why does the purpose message carry so much power at this point in time? I won't pretend to know the mind of God, but I can tell you what the Bible says. First, there's the almost unbelievable statement of Jesus recorded in John 14:12: "Very truly I tell you, whoever believes in me will do the works I have been doing, and they will do even greater things than these, because I am going to the Father." Believers have tended to ignore or dismiss that promise, or at least restrict it to supernatural signs and wonders like raising the dead or other dramatic expression of God's healing power.

Yet when you think of it, Jesus never founded a hospital, never wrote a book, never opened an orphanage, never started a school. He left those things for us to do in the power of the Spirit that He would send. I maintain that it would be as dramatic a miracle for someone like you to do any of those things just mentioned as to raise the dead. And you can only realize those kind of supernatural results that exceed what Jesus did if and when you find and flow in your God-given purpose.

Then there's the other promise in the next two verses concerning prayer in the context of doing greater things: "And I will do whatever you ask in my name, so that the Father may be glorified in the Son. You may ask me for anything in my name, and I will do it." Those verses and others like them led to the "name it and claim it" movement that stated (and I'm being simplistic here) if you can think about and ask for something, God will provide, especially prosperity, for the asker. That never seemed to work for me, so I categorized that verse along with the greater things promise as something that I would not see in my lifetime. They were only promises for a select few.

Yet, if God wants you to fulfill your purpose, and He does, then He must provide the resources to do it. If He promises that you will do greater things, He must provide what you need to do them. In other words, when you pray in your purpose, which is God's will for your life, He will provide what you need to get the job done. Therefore, the purpose message can transform your prayer life from a prayer list of those to bless and save to one that allows you to obtain answers to prayers that make a difference in your life and the lives of others.

The Apostle Paul is a good example of the power of purpose and purposeful prayers:

> I became a servant of this gospel by the gift of God's grace given me through the working of his power. Although I am less than the least of all the Lord's people, this grace was given me: to preach to the Gentiles the boundless riches of Christ, and to make plain to

everyone the administration of this mystery, which for ages past was kept hidden in God, who created all things. His intent was that now, through the church, the manifold wisdom of God should be made known to the rulers and authorities in the heavenly realms, according to his eternal purpose that he accomplished in Christ Jesus our Lord. In him and through faith in him we may approach God with freedom and confidence (Ephesians 3:7-12).

Paul's purpose was to take the gospel to the Gentiles which he claimed he did in the "working of his power." The Greek word for *working* is the same word from which we get our English word *energy*. Therefore, Paul fulfilled his purpose with divine energy. What's more, he said that through faith we all may approach God with "freedom and confidence." We can ask for what we need to do His will and He will provide, which is a summary of what Jesus said in John 14.

I can testify to the fact that I've felt and benefitted from that same kind of divine purpose energy as I have traveled, written, and consulted to express my purpose of creating order out of chaos. I've prayed and God has provided what I've

PURPOSE REVIVAL

needed. I'm increasingly aware that there's no lack or limitation in or with God; if there are any limitations, they're in my own mind.

Now it's your turn. I want you to experience this same kind of energy that empowers purposeful people, which is the reason for this book. What follows are 62 entries in no particular order, and there's no special reason for the number except that I had 62 devotionals devoted to purpose in my book *Life Is a Goldmine: Can You Dig It? Devotional.* I decided to "borrow" those entries so I edited and transferred all 62 into this book with the intent that they be read at the end of a year and the beginning of a new one in December and January so you can get your year started off with purpose power.

However, I realize you may not want or need to read them, so therefore I have included day one, day two, etc. designations to go along with the December/January dates. Each entry starts with a verse or passage, then has some narrative, and ends with a prayer. Again, the goal is to help you remove the obstacles in your mind that are keeping you from doing the greater things Jesus promised you would do.

I also recommend you work your way through this book with a journal at hand to record your thoughts and impressions. As one of the devotionals states, it's important you learn to pay attention to the little things, like enthusiasm, joy, and the still, small voice that's trying to help you recognize when you are in purposeful activity. Unless you record it when you feel it, it's trail will probably have gone cold if you try to retrieve it later.

As mentioned, I have developed many other purpose resources over the years which you can access to help you in your quest. Some of them are in book form, while others are video and audio presentations available through my website or mobile app. All those will be listed at the end, so if you want or need more of a purpose injection, they're yours for the taking.

So now, let's get started with *Purpose Revival: Learning How to Do the Greater Things*. I'm confident that the same dynamic I've experienced in my personal ministry will be yours as you work your way through these entries. May the God of your purpose guide your way as you read and reflect.

John Stanko
Pittsburgh, PA
December 2022

STOP TO-DO LIST

"In those days when the number of disciples was increasing, the Hellenistic Jews among them complained against the Hebraic Jews because their widows were being overlooked in the daily distribution of food" - Acts 6:1.

In today's verse, the leadership of the early church was faced with a good problem, but a problem nonetheless: the early church was growing. Whenever you have personal growth, or growth in your organization, it presents new opportunities and problems.

That means you must regularly make decisions about where to invest your limited time and energy. Your job will be to evaluate your "world" to see what you can stop doing, what you can

delegate, or what you should keep on doing. That can be a difficult task, but it's critical for your on-going effectiveness.

As you start a New Year or simply look to start over regardless of the time of year, are you spread too thin? Have you changed and adapted with changing conditions in your work or ministry world? What can you stop doing so you can start doing more of what you do best?

Lord, in a sense, I have become a victim of my own success. I have tried to take on more and more work and responsibility, but now I'm overwhelmed and becoming ineffective. Help me know what to stop doing and give me the courage to actually create a stop to-do list!

PURPOSE REVIVAL

YOUR YES

"So the Twelve gathered all the disciples together and said, 'It would not be right for us to neglect the ministry of the word of God in order to wait on tables'" - Acts 6:2.

The apostles were able to say no to this request for their involvement because they knew what the yes was, which of course was their purpose. And because they knew their yes, they knew it would be wrong to get involved in helping the widows, even though helping the widows was important work.

Effective people must learn to live with their limitations, even when those limitations mean they cannot help those whom they work with or care for.

Are there good, or even noble, activities that are wrong for you? Do you know to what you should say no because you know what your yes is? Can you say no without feeling guilty? Do you keep saying yes hoping to find your purpose in one of them?

Lord, I need Your light and insight to understand what my purpose is. Then I need the courage to say no to requests to do things not connected to my purpose, just like the apostles did.

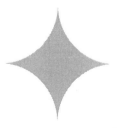

DAY 3

TRUST OTHERS

"Brothers and sisters, choose seven men from among you who are known to be full of the Spirit and wisdom. We will turn this responsibility over to them and will give our attention to prayer and the ministry of the word" - Acts 6:3-4.

The apostles devised a plan that enabled the problem to be resolved with minimum effort on their part. When you let go of doing things you are emotionally or professionally attached to doing or being, you must find and trust others who will have the same commitment as you.

Therefore, you don't stop doing things by giving them to just anyone, but you still must find a way to stop doing them nonetheless. What's more, you have to be training your replacement(s)

whenever you can so you have others you trust and to whom you can delegate.

Do you struggle with letting go? Is changing roles difficult for you? Have you worked to train others so they will carry tasks out with your same high standards (even your children)? What's keeping you from making these shifts in your role and duties?

Lord, my lack of trust in others is really a lack of trust in You. If You equipped me to do things, You can equip others to do them just as well or better. I release my roles and responsibilities to You, so I can embrace the new things You have for me. Help me learn to trust You and others!

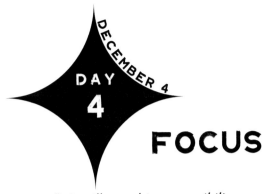

FOCUS

*"We will turn this responsibility over
to them and will give our attention to
prayer and the ministry of the word"*
- Acts 6:4.

The apostles kept their focus on what they did best, what Jesus assigned them to do: pray and tell others about Him. The goal in delegating is to have others do what they can do well so you can focus on what only you can do well.

When the apostles prayed, buildings shook. When they ministered the Word, many came to know Jesus. If you have people who can produce results, and if you can produce specific results, then everyone needs to be doing the things to get those results.

What is it that you do that "shakes buildings?" Is it art? Listening? Fixing broken

things? Healing the sick? Whatever it is, stop doing whatever you can in order to invest more time in your purpose, gifts, and goals.

Lord, I don't see how I can stop doing some things to more effectively do the things I love and am gifted to do. Help me see my world as You see it, realizing that if I died tomorrow, someone would have to start doing what I do. Help me have that kind of urgency surrounding my purpose while yet living.

PURPOSE REVIVAL

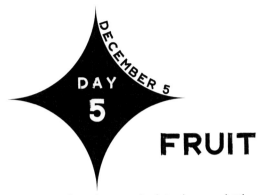

FRUIT

"So the word of God spread. The number of disciples in Jerusalem increased rapidly, and a large number of priests became obedient to the faith" - Acts 6:7.

The apostles were interested in one thing: fruit where the gospel was concerned. God's ways are ultimately effective and will lead to productive labor. He may put you through a season of training where you don't see results, but that's the exception and not the rule. He wants you to fulfill your purpose more than you do, and will partner with you so that you have some measure of success in what it is He created you to do.

Are you happy with the fruit of purpose in your life? Are you afraid of or ambivalent about purpose results? Do you explain away

your lack of results, saying it's not the will of God for you or the right season? Part of your lack of fruit may be that you are engaged in good activities but not the correct activities that will enable you to produce results.

Lord, You desire for all Your disciples to bear fruit that will remain. I'm Your disciple, so You expect fruit from my efforts. I'll no longer be happy with trying hard, nor will I spin my lack of results to make me feel good when the fruit isn't there. Help me see where my fruitful labor is.

DECEMBER 6

DAY 6

POTENTIAL

"I am a Jew, born in Tarsus of Cilicia, but brought up in this city. I studied under Gamaliel and was thoroughly trained in the law of our ancestors. I was just as zealous for God as any of you are today" - Acts 22:3.

When Paul thought he knew his purpose as a Jew, he pursued it with great zeal and found the best mentor and training he could find. This all came in handy later when his purpose was adjusted to be an apostle.

In other words, God can't promote potential. He can only promote those who have developed their potential to the fullest. Training and education are a big part of that development, for God can't get out of you what someone else didn't put in you in the first place.

What are you doing to develop your purpose or what you think is your purpose? Are you seeking training and education as part of that development? Is reading a part of that development plan? What else can you do to get ready for your purpose debut?

Lord, I want to be the fullest, best expression of who You created me to be. Therefore, I need and want the training, knowledge, and skill that will make that happen. Send me opportunities and people to develop my potential, and I commit to do the work to become world-class in my particular purpose expression.

PURPOSE REVIVAL

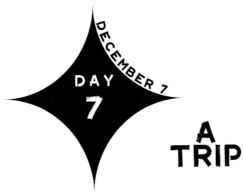

A TRIP

*"Jesus and his disciples went on to
the villages around Caesarea Philippi.
On the way he asked them, 'Who do
people say I am?'" - Mark 8:27.*

When God wants to speak to you, He often
takes you on a trip. When you're out of your usual
daily routine, you're more open to the things around
you and that also means you're more open to the
Lord. This is exactly what was happening in this verse.

Jesus took the disciples far away from the
hustle and bustle of Galilee and Jerusalem to a remote area to talk to them about who He was and
to warn them about His future suffering.

It was on this trip that Peter found his purpose (he was given the keys to the Kingdom) and
the disciples discovered who Jesus was in a whole
new way!

JOHN W. STANKO   13

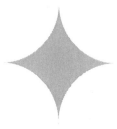

Is it time that you take a few days and go off with the Lord? What will you talk to Him about when you go? What questions will you ask?

Lord, I need some time with You, just You and me, talking about Your will and purpose for my life. I pray You would create some time in my schedule that I can make that happen. When I arrive for our appointment, I'll be open to whatever You choose to say and show me.

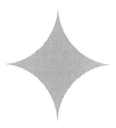

PURPOSE REVIVAL

CLARITY

"In Joppa there was a disciple named Tabitha (in Greek her name is Dorcas); she was always doing good and helping the poor"
- Acts 9:36, emphasis added.

This woman named Dorcas had a personal purpose to care for the poor in a specific venue. Everyone else in the village saw the needs she saw, but only she was moved to action because God had created her to help the poor.

Notice the clarity and simplicity of her purpose—just a few words that described what she best did most often to do good and help the poor.

Do you have this kind of clarity? Do you make your purpose quest too complicated? Are you, in reality, so close to your situation

that you can't be objective? Do you need some-one to help clarify your purpose?

Lord, I have a purpose and I can see that it's simple and been with me most of my life. Help me see and describe it with a few words that explode with meaning, just like they did for Dorcas. Help me also to move past my wrong thinking that may cloud my perspective of who I am in Your eyes.

DAY
9

DECEMBER 9

EVIDENCE

"Peter went with them, and when he arrived he was taken upstairs to the room. All the widows stood around him, crying and showing him the robes and other clothing that Dorcas had made while she was still with them" - Acts 9:39.

When Peter arrived on the scene, the evidence of Tabitha's life purpose interceded on her behalf! The widows missed her, and they showed Peter all the garments she had made for them while she was alive.

Tabitha didn't just talk about what she was going to do; she did it. If she was alive today, she would have a sewing machine and a source of material and cloth, and would be sewing for the poor day and night.

Do you talk about what you're going to do one day? Are you pursuing your purpose, whether you can make any money from it or not? What more can you do than what you're currently doing?

Lord, I'm a good talker but not always a good doer. I'm often hesitant and don't know how to start, or I've started but then don't know how to finish. Help me, Lord, to find strategies that will enable me to assemble a body of purpose evidence capable of representing me before You in my day of trouble as it did for Dorcas.

DAY 10

HEAVEN'S RESOURCES

"Peter sent them all out of the room; then he got down on his knees and prayed. Turning toward the dead woman, he said, 'Tabitha, get up.' She opened her eyes, and seeing Peter she sat up"
- Acts 9:40.

In this story, it's easy to put the focus on Peter, for God used him to perform a great miracle. However, let's take a moment and look at it from Tabitha's perspective. Here was an insignificant woman ministering to insignificant people in a small, nowhere town, but in her day of trouble, when she couldn't cry out for herself, the evidence of a life yielded to God's purpose cried out for her. And the most significant spiritual leader in the world at that time came to her rescue!

When you're functioning in purpose, all the

resources of heaven are at your disposal because God is watching and protecting your purpose.

Are you praying like this is so? What do you need to make your purpose more effective? Why not pray for that today, and then thank God for it like you already have it (ask and give thanks)? What or where is your body of purpose evidence?

Lord, at times I'm guilty of asking for too little, acting like I will deplete Your supply of something if I ask for too much. Yet You have something for me to do and I need Your help and provision to do it. I ask You for the resources necessary to do Your will and I thank You in advance for Your provision.

PURPOSE REVIVAL

DAY
11
A MAN NAMED NEHEMIAH

"The men of Jericho built the adjoining section, and Zakkur son of Imri built next to them. The Fish Gate was rebuilt by the sons of Hassenaah. They laid its beams and put its doors and bolts and bars in place"
- Nehemiah 3:2-3.

Nehemiah's purpose was to rebuild Jerusalem, a big task that was to involve many people—some friendly to his cause, some not. He had to give significant thought to how he was going to organize his effort, and the decisions in these verses provide just a glimpse from God's inspired Word of who did what to rebuild the wall, the first step in Nehemiah's purpose plan.

What thought have you given to how you'll achieve your purpose work? How are

you organizing your world to make it happen? What changes do you need to make to be more effective and fruitful?

Lord, I've had big dreams and plans, but often they break down in the implementation phase. In other words, I haven't known how, and sometimes not wanted to know how, to make the changes necessary to rearrange my world to fulfill my purpose. Help me to do so and help me to help others do so as well.

PURPOSE REVIVAL

PURPOSE LIGHT

"So then, King Agrippa, I was not disobedient to the vision from heaven" - Acts 26:19.

Paul found his purpose on the Damascus Road and called it a vision from heaven. The light he received that day was brighter than the noon-day sun in the Middle East. That's the kind of intense and focused light God can shine on His will for your life so you can see what it is.

What's more, Paul stated that he was not disobedient to that heavenly vision, which indicates it's possible to ignore or disobey God's purpose for your life. Paul chose not to do so.

What light has God given you concerning His will for your life? Are you stalling or putting off embracing that will? Are you acting like there's no need for urgency to fulfilling your purpose?

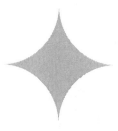

Lord, I accept Your will for my life. I won't run away or delay, but will do just what Paul did, and that was to accept Your will and partner with You to fulfill it. I put my trust in You for finances, wisdom, and power to be effective and efficient in my own personal vision from heaven.

COMPLIMENTS

"'Get up,' the Lord said, 'and go into Damascus. There you will be told all that you have been assigned to do'"
- Acts 22:10.

Paul had an assignment and God took him to a place where someone would describe and confirm what that assignment was. God wants you to know your purpose and often sends people to provide clues and specific direction where your purpose is concerned.

That often comes in the form of feedback and compliments, which you can easily ignore or misread. It should not surprise you that God speaks to you, for He is a great communicator and wants you to know your purpose. All you have to do is pay attention and have faith in His ability to send you a message.

Is there any compliment you've heard regularly that may be a key to your purpose? Why not ask some others to share with you what they see to be your strengths that may indicate purpose? Better yet, why not ask God and have faith He will answer?

Lord, I'm open to hear what my purpose is from others, who may not have the bias I have towards who I am. Show me who I can ask and then give them Your insight that will help me know and do Your will for my life. Also, show me anything others have regularly told me that I now see is an indication of my purpose.

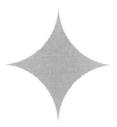

PURPOSE REVIVAL

DECEMBER 14

DAY 14

YOUR FUTURE

"When I returned to Jerusalem and was praying at the temple, I fell into a trance and saw the Lord speaking to me. 'Quick!' he said. 'Leave Jerusalem immediately, because the people here will not accept your testimony about me'" - Acts 22:17-18.

God understands your purpose and knows how people will respond to your presence and work. Here He directed Paul to leave working among his beloved fellow Jews to go to the Gentiles, because the Lord knew the Jews would not accept Paul's testimony.

God not only assigns your purpose but also becomes your purpose coach, directing your steps and development along the way. He also assigns where you will be most fruitful

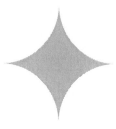

Are you cooperating with God's plan for your purpose, which may include school, being coached and trained, and travel? Are you trying to choose where you will be effective, or surrendering to the reality of where you get the greatest results?

Lord, You know best because You see the future and can direct my steps today to make sure I'm ready to meet the challenges of tomorrow. I accept Your guidance and wisdom, and will no longer fight what I must do to be successful in my purpose. I start or continue today to develop myself into Your purpose champion.

FATHER KNOWS BEST

"'Lord,' I replied, 'these people know that I went from one synagogue to another to imprison and beat those who believe in you'" - Acts 22:19.

When the Lord told Paul to leave Jerusalem, Paul objected, reasoning with the Lord that it made more sense for him to stay. Paul thought the people would recognize his conversion and repentance and accept his testimony.

In other words, Paul didn't want to go, but rather wanted to choose his own purpose, or at least his purpose sphere of influence. The Lord made it easy for him, however, for Paul could either depart or stay and die at the hands of his countrymen.

Are you resisting your purpose, holding out for what you want to do? If so, then you're

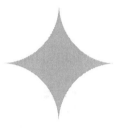

missing some of the abundant life that can be yours, and you need to surrender to God's plan if you want purpose success.

Lord, there are times when I've felt I knew better than You know what my purpose should be and where it should be expressed. I ask Your forgiveness for trying to run my life and I surrender today to Your purpose and plan. I'll go where You want me to go and do what You want me to do. Show me what and where that is.

PURPOSE REVIVAL

SPHERE OF INFLUENCE

"Then the Lord said to me, 'Go; I will send you far away to the Gentiles'" - Acts 22:21.

You can't say, "God, I'll do whatever You want as long as it's in this country, in this city, on this street, with these people, in this building, and on these days." God assigns not only your purpose but also your sphere of influence where and among whom your purpose will flourish and be most productive.

You'll know where you're supposed to express your purpose because it's the place where you're celebrated and not only tolerated, or worse yet, ignored. God isn't trying to trick you; He wants you to know.

Do you know your sphere of influence? Among what group or in what setting are you most effective? Are you functioning in

it? If not, why not? Of what or whom are you afraid?

Lord, I have an idea of where I'm most effective, but I'm dragging my feet. I'm scared and I don't know how that will work out with my current responsibilities and duties. Help me accept my sphere of influence and give me strategies to carry out my duties there.

PURPOSE REVIVAL

GOD'S CALL

"And the Lord said to Moses, 'See, I have called by name Bezalel son of Uri, the son of Hur, of the tribe of Judah'" - Exodus 31:1-2 (AMP).

When you're called, it means God has spoken your name and you'll hear something that's meant only for you. Purpose is a message from your heavenly headquarters with your name on it. God had you specifically in mind for the job and no one can fulfill it as well as you can.

What's more, God will speak and reveal your purpose to others so they know what it is and can help open doors for you. If they can't see it, they'll at least see the results and expect you to produce them.

Do you have a sense of calling in your daily work? If not, what's the voice of God calling

you to do? How can you expect your purpose to be clear to others if it's not clear to you? Is it clear to others but you're resisting what they have been telling you?

Lord, I want this sense of calling in my daily work. I'll no longer be content just to be part of a group, but I'll seek after a sense of individual purpose in my life. I trust that You will speak clearly to me, for my heart is tuned to hear You call my name where purpose is concerned. Speak, Lord, for Your servant listens!

PURPOSE REVIVAL

SECOND-NATURE

"And I have filled him with the Spirit of God, with wisdom, with understanding, with knowledge and with all kinds of skills" - Exodus 31:3.

The Lord filled Bezalel with all kinds of skills in a specific area and the same is true for you. These skills can seem so natural for you that it causes you to look past them as you search for purpose.

What's more, they can seem rather unspiritual when you consider that you do simple everyday things like listen, teach, play with children, organize household items, or remember names and people's stories quite easily. Yet all those things have been deposited in you by God's Spirit, so they all mean something as you seek to clarify your purpose.

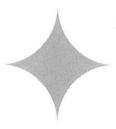

Why not make a list today of all the skills you have, no matter how basic? Perhaps you can employ the help of others as you do? Then study the list to see if there are any connections or clues to help you clarify your purpose.

Lord, it's difficult for me to see myself, but I want to recognize and acknowledge all the good skills with which Your Spirit has filled me. Show me who I am today. Don't let me look past those things that seem simple or second-nature to me, for You put them there for a reason.

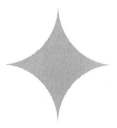

PURPOSE REVIVAL

HANDIWORK

*". . . to make artistic designs for work
in gold, silver and bronze, to cut and
set stones, to work in wood, and to
engage in all kinds of crafts"*
- Exodus 31:4-5.

God filled Bezalel with His Spirit, not to perform church duties like preaching, teaching, or counseling. He filled him so he could work with his hands and produce items from wood, metal, and cloth. Bezalel's purpose was to work in his shop to produce works of art for the Lord. Then God assigned him important work on the tabernacle because Bezalel was gifted and had developed that gift.

Did you ever consider that your artistic abilities are more than just a family trait or personal interest, but are instead initiated and

inspired by God's Spirit? When you crochet, paint, make jewelry, or sew, do you see yourself performing spiritual activities? Maybe it's time to consider your artistic endeavors to be more than just a hobby or side interest?

Lord, there are times when I haven't considered my artistic talents to be special, let alone inspired by Your Spirit. I accept these talents as Your gifts to me and the world around me, and I ask You for help to make them all they can be so I can do Your work and fulfill my purpose.

HELPERS

"Moreover, I have appointed Oholiab son of Ahisamak, of the tribe of Dan, to help him. Also I have given ability to all the skilled workers to make everything I have commanded you"
- Exodus 31:6.

God didn't create you capable of doing everything. When you know your purpose, you realize your need to be part of a team, whether in a family or at work or in ministry. That way you can do what only you can do and others can do the same.

Bezalel was the chief artisan, but God gave him a group of others who could perform at a high level and were capable of undergirding the work God had given Bezalel to do.

Who are your team members? Of which team are you a part? What do you bring to the team? What do others bring? How well are you working as a team?

Lord, I'm coming to realize my limitations as well as my strengths. I see that I need to be part of a team in most everything I do, even though working with others can be difficult and sometimes painful. Show me how I can be a contributing member of an effective team to enhance my purpose work.

PURPOSE REVIVAL

GOD'S EYES

"They are to make them just as I commanded you" - Exodus 31:11.

The craftsmen, who were filled with God's Spirit to perform their duties, made the things for the tabernacle as the Lord directed them through Moses. In other words, God directed their purpose through their leader.

What's more, some of what they made was seen by all and some was seen only by the high priest and God Himself! Your purpose may be public or it may be something you do for God's eyes only. Either way, it's unique to you and you must treat it as the treasure it is.

What has God filled you with His purpose to do? Who helps direct your purpose? Is your purpose more public or private? Do you value what you do and who you are? If you

don't value what you have, then how will others be expected to recognize and value it?

Lord, my purpose is an assignment from You, but You may use others to help direct my purpose expressions. You may also have me do things that most people don't see or notice, but I know You notice them. I accept these limitations and commit to give my all no matter what, even if only Your eyes can see the work I'm doing.

DECEMBER 22

DAY
22

WHAT, NOT HOW

*"Moses thought that his own people
would realize that God was using him
to rescue them, but they did not"
- Acts 7:25.*

According to Stephen in Acts 7, Moses knew his purpose was to rescue the Jews who were in Egypt. Moses assumed everyone else knew that too, but they didn't. As Moses tried to fulfill His purpose, first Moses killed an Egyptian and hid the body. Then he tried to be an arbiter and judge, counseling his people to stop fighting with one another. Moses knew *what* he was supposed to do with his life, but he didn't understand *how* he was to do it. This led him to do things that were not consistent with how he would ultimately rescue his people in the fullness of God's power.

Do you know what you are supposed to do? Are you taking time to prepare yourself and see the strategy for how you will do it? This waiting on the strategy should not be passive, however, but is a time of spiritual and practical preparation.

Lord, I don't want to wait to fulfill my purpose, but I need You to show me how to prepare and how to do it. I don't want to sit, but I don't want to step out like Moses and do wrong things. Help me know how to do what it is You want me to do, and I promise I will aggressively pursue it.

PURPOSE REVIVAL

FLOATING ON PURPOSE

"At that time Moses was born, and he was no ordinary child. For three months he was cared for by his family" - Acts 7:20.

All newborns look pretty much alike, but Moses' parents saw something in their baby boy that was different. What did they see? They saw purpose! While all the other baby boys were being thrown into the river according to Pharaoh's decree, Moses' family kept theirs for as long as they could.

Then they complied with the edict, the only difference being that they first put him in a floating basket. From there, Moses' purpose kept him safe and directed him into Pharaoh's household. That's an indication of the power of purpose, and God's desire to direct, preserve, and release it.

If you have children in your family or work with kids, what do you see? Do you see the problems or the potential? Have you released those children to find and fulfill God's will and purpose for their lives rather than your own interpretation of what they should do?

Lord, I thank You for the children in my life. At times, I tend to look at their weaknesses and not their purpose. Help me to see that clearly and then help me know what I can do to encourage and develop their potential. Finally, give me grace to release them so they can float on the flow of their purpose to where they need to be, just like Moses did with his.

PURPOSEFUL TEAMS

"On the contrary, they recognized that I had been entrusted with the task of preaching the gospel to the uncircumcised, just as Peter had been to the circumcised" - Galatians 2:7.

It's important you know your purpose so you can tell others what you do best. It's just as important to know the purpose of others, so you can know where their shoulders are broadest, so to speak, and where you can rely on them the most.

Paul knew Peter's purpose. Peter knew Paul's. The other apostles knew Peter's and Paul's. That's why the early church grew, for everyone functioned in their purpose and gifts as God empowered them to be successful.

Do you know your purpose? Can you describe it to those with whom you work, live,

and/or minister? Do you know the purpose of those around you? Do you take time to ask and listen to learn both theirs and your own?

Lord, I need clarity of purpose so I can know what I have to offer my family, work team, and church. I need the same kind of clarity to know the purpose of my spouse, children, co-workers, and team members. Make every team I'm part of a well-oiled machine that can do great things for You in the power of each one's purpose.

PURPOSE REVIVAL

DECEMBER 25

DAY
25

REASSURANCE

"One night the Lord spoke to Paul in a vision: 'Do not be afraid; keep on speaking, do not be silent'"
- Acts 18:9.

Someone once said when the Lord tells you not to be afraid, it's usually too late! It's hard to imagine Paul being afraid, but in this instance he was. The Lord appeared to reassure him that he was doing well and that God would protect him.

Your purpose can be a fearful thing because it seems so big and because you don't know how you'll achieve it. God may also send you to do what you do best in a place that's completely out of your comfort zone. Don't expect God to reassure you, however, unless you're *doing* something about and with your purpose.

Are you afraid of your purpose? Of what specifically are you fearful? Are you expecting some encouragement when you aren't really engaged in your purpose? Do you see that encouragement is something you earn by attempting to be fruitful?

Lord, I'm afraid of many things: what others think, failure, success, poverty, and personal growth. I'm not asking for another confirmation of what I am to do, but I'm asking that You affirm and encourage me today and every day—but only as I take steps that lead to purpose.

DECEMBER 26

DAY
26

ENCOURAGEMENT

"Last night an angel of the God to whom I belong and whom I serve stood beside me and said, 'Do not be afraid, Paul. You must stand trial before Caesar; and God has graciously given you the lives of all who sail with you'" - Acts 27:23-24.

When all on the ship to Rome appeared lost, an angel appeared to Paul, reminding Him of God's promise that he would witness to Caesar. Paul in turn encouraged everyone else with the words with which God had encouraged him.

When you're functioning in purpose, God will provide abundant grace that helps and encourages you. This comfort will then be a source of encouragement to others as you share it with them.

Are you giving your all to your purpose? Or are you sitting on the sidelines in fear, hoping God will do for you what only you can do for yourself, which is obey His will for your life?

Lord, I crave Your encouragement, but I know I can only receive it when I have earned it. I earn it by obediently taking steps to complete the purpose assignment You have given me. Forgive me for waiting for You to do what You expect me to do, and that's to act in purposeful faith and hope.

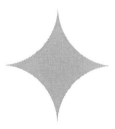

PURPOSE REVIVAL

DAY 27

LOOKING FOR YOU

"For two whole years Paul stayed there in his own rented house and welcomed all who came to see him. He proclaimed the kingdom of God and taught about the Lord Jesus Christ—with all boldness and without hindrance!" - Acts 28:30-31.

After all Paul had been through and even though he was a chained prisoner in Rome, God was with him to fulfill his purpose. He did not have to go looking for people to whom he could preach; they came looking for him, right to his very home!

What's more, tradition has it that Paul led every one of his Roman guards to Jesus. That's the power of purpose; you don't have to go looking for it, it comes looking for you.

What group of people or activity always seem to find you, even if you're in a crowd? What need presents itself to you regularly so you can provide the answer or cure?

Lord, I acknowledge that I have a purpose! Sometimes, however, it's difficult to see because it's so second nature to me. Help me recognize what always seems to find me, and then help me make sense out of that to define my purpose. Once I see and say it, help me be bold to do it, just like Paul was bold in Rome.

PURPOSE REVIVAL

YOUR JOY, NOT YOUR JOB

"There he met a Jew named Aquila, a native of Pontus, who had recently come from Italy with his wife Priscilla, because Claudius had ordered all Jews to leave Rome. Paul went to see them, and because he was a tentmaker as they were, he stayed and worked with them" - Acts 18:2-3.

Paul wrote 13 letters, but never once told us what he did to make money. Yet in every letter he told us about his purpose. Paul didn't take his identity from what he did to make money, but rather from what he did that gave him the greatest fulfillment, which was the gospel to the Gentiles. You may or may not make money from your purpose, but it's the main reason you're here and alive.

Have you been defining yourself by your occupation instead of purpose? If you're

frustrated with your job, what can you do after work that's purpose-related? Are you preoccupied with how you can make money from your purpose, which is keeping you from doing it?

Lord, I thank You for Your provision, but often my work isn't a good expression of who I am. Yet my culture urges me to define myself by what I do for a living. Help me be free from this thinking and to see my purpose in a new light so I can describe myself to others and myself by my joy and not my job.

PURPOSE REVIVAL

A DIFFERENT PERSPECTIVE

*"Our dear friend Luke, the doctor,
and Demas send greetings"*
- Colossians 4:14.

Luke reported what Paul did to make money in Acts and Paul returned the favor by telling us what Luke did in Colossians. Neither man introduced or identified himself by what he did to earn a living, but by what he did that gave him joy and expressed his purpose in God's kingdom.

If you love missions but sell insurance, for example, perhaps you should follow Paul and Luke's examples and introduce yourself as a missionary, even if you only go into the mission field for a few weeks every year.

How do you see yourself where money, occupation, and purpose are concerned? What identity is uppermost in your mind? Do you

JOHN W. STANKO   57

need a change of thinking and perspective on this matter?

Lord, if I keep on doing and thinking as I always have, I'll continue to get the same results. I need to see my life, work, and world differently, and I need Your help to do so. Help me see myself from a purpose perspective and then give me the courage to state that to the world, not fearing criticism or ridicule.

PURPOSE REVIVAL

DAY
30

DECEMBER 30

DIVINE ENERGY

*"I became a servant of this gospel
by the gift of God's grace given me
through the working of his power"*
- Ephesians 3:7.

As I pointed out in the Introduction, the word for *working* here is derived from the Greek *energeo*, from which the English word energy comes. Your purpose is a gift and it comes through a divine working of His power in you. It also energizes you, so much so that you can lose sleep and not eat while functioning in purpose and still be effective, enthusiastic, and joyful.

What are you energized to do? When do you sense God's energy flowing with and through you? What can you do and forget to eat or lose track of what time it is?

Lord, I thank You for my purpose, even though I can't see all of what it is right now. I also thank You for Your divine energy and power that work through me in purpose, even if I'm not clear what that purpose is. I trust You will show me my purpose and also pray You will help me see where Your energy flows most abundantly in my life.

PURPOSE REVIVAL

DAY
31

DECEMBER 31

LIFE PATTERNS

"Jacob's well was there, and Jesus, tired as he was from the journey, sat down by the well. It was about noon. When a Samaritan woman came to draw water, Jesus said to her, 'Will you give me a drink?'" - John 4:6-7.

Jesus sat down to rest and wait for lunch, but the Father had other ideas and brought a needy woman to Him. Jesus looked past His own needs to meet the needs of this woman and He had a fruitful exchange that changed her life.

You seldom have to go looking for purpose, it almost always comes looking for you. God wants you to fulfill your purpose more than you do and that's why He brings opportunities, people, and situations across your path.

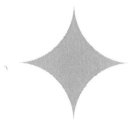

Think about your life as far back as possible and ask yourself what situations have repeatedly sought you out to be involved? What scenario or problem always finds you because you can help or have some answers?

Lord, I know You aren't trying to trick me by bringing things into my life just to test whether or not I will or will not engage them. Help me to see any life patterns of things that always seem to find me to be involved because You want me involved. Help me not to miss anything so I can recognize my purpose.

PURPOSE REVIVAL

DABBLING

*"Let your eyes look straight ahead; fix
your gaze directly before you"*
- Proverbs 4:25.

Purpose requires a singular focus if you're
going to bear fruit, especially when you're em-
ployed in something not related to your purpose.
Your purpose may not begin until 5:01 when the
work day ends, and you must be ready to go back
to work at purpose after work-for-pay is done.

The evangelist, Dwight L. Moody, said,
"This one thing I do, not these many things I dab-
ble in." We can be great dabblers, for it keeps us
from being accountable for the one thing we were
created to do.

**Are you a dabbler? Is your focus singular,
or are you distracted with many cares and interests? Where do you invest your energy and**

creative expression? What can you do to improve your focus?

Lord, I don't want to be a dabbler, doing a little of this and that, being effective at nothing. I want to know my purpose and then structure my life and world to fulfill it. Give me the courage to say 'no' to the things that are a distraction, even if they're noble and can make me some money.

PURPOSE REVIVAL

PASSIVE/ AGGRESSIVE

"Give careful thought to the paths for your feet and be steadfast in all your ways" - Proverbs 4:26.

There's an old proverb that states, "Some people make things happen, some watch them happen, and some say, 'What happened?'" Where purpose is concerned, you *must* take steps to make things happen, all the while trusting the Lord to open doors while you try the door knobs and ring the door bells. Once you set your purpose path after careful thought and prayer, you must be steadfast and not give up.

Are you waiting for things to happen and not being proactive? Are you passive when you should be aggressive? Are you discouraged and thus inactive and ineffective?

Lord, it seems that progress can be slow where purpose is concerned. Then there's confusion over when I should act and when I should wait on You before I act. Give me clarity of thought as I consider my way and then a hearty spirit to endure the trials along the way. Help me know my role in the purpose process and progress.

PURPOSE REVIVAL

THE DISTRACTION LANE

*"Do not turn to the right or the left;
keep your foot from evil"*
- Proverbs 24:7.

Purpose and goals require you to focus on the matters at hand and resist all temptations to wander down the path labeled 'distraction lane.' What's more, fear will masquerade and present all kinds of options of what you can do, so it's easy to be confused and ask, "There are so many things I *can* do, how can I be sure what it is I *should* do?"

Don't fall for that ploy. Set your goals, pursue what you understand your purpose to be at this time, and do something every day to make goals and purpose a reality.

Are you under siege by far too many thoughts and creative ideas? Is this paralyzing

you, causing you to constantly analyze things so in turn you end up doing nothing?

Lord, I thought I was just overly curious and creative, but today I see that it's a manifestation of fear that serves to keep me traveling down distraction lane, preventing me from focusing on the main things in my life. I have a good idea what I must do and today I commit to do a little something to bring me closer to purpose, creativity, and my goal fulfillment.

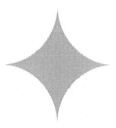

PURPOSE REVIVAL

YOUR FINGERPRINTS

"The Lord has made everything for its own purpose, even the wicked for the day of evil" - Proverbs 16:4 (NAS).

God is a God of purpose and has assigned you something to do only you can do, something for you to be only you can be. Your purpose is sort of like your spiritual fingerprints. It distinguishes you from everyone else so that when you touch something in God's will, you leave a mark that's uniquely yours.

What's more, if God wants you to fulfill your purpose—and of course He does—then He must reveal to you what His will is. He can't hold you accountable for what you do not know.

Do you know your purpose? Are you doing it, or at least making progress toward its fulfillment? What steps can you take to know

or implement your purpose from where you are now?

Lord, I know You're a God of purpose. Show me my identity and help me recognize my spiritual fingerprints. Then allow me to touch the world and leave my mark according to Your plan and will. I thirst for purpose and You are the only One who can release and empower me to find and fulfill it. Help me, I pray!

PURPOSE REVIVAL

PURPOSE SOUNDS

"Make your ear attentive to wisdom,
Incline your heart to understanding . . ."
- Proverbs 2:2.

When you seek purpose, you must be able not only to ask God for help but also to know how to listen for the sounds of purpose. This can't be a part-time pursuit, but must be an urgent desire accompanied with a sense of adventure.

God is a great communicator, and will speak to you in many ways, including through a small, still voice in your inner being. That means you must pay attention to your heart, and recognize the glimmers of joy that are always the telltale sign of purpose.

How focused are you on your purpose quest—half-hearted or all-in? What's your heart telling you today? Where are your sounds

of purposeful joy most audible in your heart and spirit that can help lead you to a knowledge of your purpose?

Lord, I confess I don't know how to listen for the sounds of purpose in my life. That sound is often the echo of joy from certain activities or people when I'm around them. Help me not to be afraid of those sounds, but to recognize them for the seismic activity that indicates an earthquake of purpose is near in my life.

HIDDEN TREASURE

*"For if you cry for discernment, Lift
your voice for understanding; If you
seek her as silver and search for her
as for hidden treasures"*
- Proverbs 2:3-4.

If you had a guarantee that there's a valuable stash of treasure buried in your backyard, what would you do? Would you only pray about it? Would you dig one hole and if you didn't find it, give up searching? Let's hope not!

You would dig and then dig some more, and then enlist some professional help, and utilize some earth-moving equipment until you found it. That's how you should look for purpose. It can't be a passive endeavor.

What are you doing to find your promised purpose? With whom are you consulting?

What are you reading? How fervently are you praying to find your purpose?

Lord, I've been guilty of waiting for purpose to come to me, instead of embarking on an all-out search like I would for hidden treasure. I see now that the search is part of Your plan to help me appreciate purpose when I find it because of the price I paid to get there. Forgive me for being passive and not doing my part, and help me see all I can do to search.

EXPECTANT LISTENING

"Then you will discern the fear of the Lord and discover the knowledge of God" - Proverbs 2:5.

When you diligently search for purpose (or for that matter anything) like you would for hidden treasure, you'll find it. God isn't hiding anything, but He does conceal it so you will search.

And when your search is finished, you'll appreciate what you have because of the price you paid to find it. You'll also be less likely to sell it cheaply because of the price you paid to get it.

Are you seeking the Lord for answers, expecting to hear? What are you doing differently that can give you the results you desire where hearing is concerned? Are you acting on what you hear or waiting for more and more confirmation?

JOHN W. STANKO   75

Lord, I know You want me to do Your will, so I know You'll reveal Your will to me if I ask. Your Word clearly states that I'll receive if I ask and don't doubt. I'm asking You for wisdom today— wisdom for my life and the way forward for my purpose. I expect to hear an answer today, and I commit to act on that answer without wavering.

PURPOSE REVIVAL

ENHANCED APPRECIATION

"It is the glory of God to conceal a matter, But the glory of kings is to search out a matter" - Proverbs 25:2.

As you learned yesterday, God isn't teasing you when He requires you to search for purpose. The higher the price you pay for it, the greater the value it has when you find it. This is called enhanced appreciation, and is part of your preparation to fulfill your purpose, for it will require the same (maybe more) diligence and patience to see your purpose expressed as it did to discover it in the first place.

Do you see the value in searching diligently for purpose? Do you understand this is part of the process as you develop your seeking skills? Are you ready today to redouble your efforts to find and fulfill your purpose?

Lord, You know what You're doing. If You're concealing purpose from me right now, it's because I'm not ready to see it, or You know I need to develop myself through the seeking process. I submit to this process and commit to enjoy the search, for it will lead to an enhanced appreciation of what I have when I find it.

PURPOSE
TEAM

*"He who separates himself seeks his
own desire, he quarrels against all
sound wisdom"*
- Proverbs 18:1 (NAS).

You usually won't find or fulfill your purpose and goals in isolation. Others will help sharpen your focus and see what you can't see for whatever reason. While you must judge and evaluate what others say, you should not dismiss it out of hand, especially if you have heard the same feedback or comments from more than a few people.

Who's part of your purpose support group that can help you clarify your purpose and then keep you on track? Among whom are you making your purpose known so you can bless and serve them? Do you know the

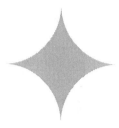

purpose of other people so you can complement them as you serve together in some noble task?

*Lord, working with others can be difficult. I
suppose that's why You commanded us so often
to forgive others. Help me find a team where I
can be who I am and they can be who they are
so together we can see supernatural results as
we work together in our daily expressions of
purpose.*

ABUNDANCE

"Those who work their land will have abundant food, but those who chase fantasies will have their fill of poverty" - Proverbs 28:19.

A fantasy is anything that isn't based in reality. When you try to be who you aren't, or do what you were never meant to do, you'll experience lack because you're pursuing something that isn't based in reality. That lack you experience may be energy, creativity, time, and/or money. When you work your land, however, there's always a bumper crop of fruit.

Where are you chasing fantasies? Where and what is your land that produces the greatest amount of fruit and opportunities? If you're experiencing lack right now, could it be because you're not working your God-assigned land?

JOHN W. STANKO

81

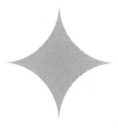

Lord, deliver me from fantasies that include who I think You want me to be, who others want me to be, or what my current job or role demands of me to be. I want to be who I am and work my land so I can experience an abundance of joy, fruit, and peace. I'll stake out and work my personal land today.

PURPOSE REVIVAL

PERSONAL INVESTMENT

"He who gets wisdom loves his own soul; He who keeps understanding will find good" - Proverbs 19:8.

Jesus said you must love your neighbor as yourself. To find purpose, you must believe you are worth purpose. Therefore, any low self-esteem hang-ups you have will shortcut the purpose process.

What's more, it's in your best interests to find and fulfill your purpose, for God wants to bless you through it. When you don't search or find purpose, you miss the blessing of God and hurt yourself!

Do you invest time and energy in your purpose quest? Do you believe you're worth the investment? Are there any areas in your heart working against your search, like self-hatred, bitterness, or low self-esteem?

Lord, I'm worth the investment it takes to find and fulfill purpose. You created me and then redeemed me, paying a high price in the process. Since You invested so much in me, now I want to invest in myself so You can have a return on Your investment, so to speak. I'll no longer fight the process.

PURPOSE REVIVAL

ENTRUSTMENT

"But on the contrary, seeing that I had been entrusted with the gospel to the uncircumcised, just as Peter had been to the circumcised (for He who effectually worked for Peter in his apostleship to the circumcised effectually worked for me also to the Gentiles)" - Galatians 2:7-9.

Paul knew his purpose and could express it simply and clearly (take the gospel to the uncircumcised). Peter knew his purpose and could do the same (take the gospel to the Jews). Both were so clear and precise that others could also describe each man's purpose. Notice also that Paul saw his purpose as an entrustment from the Lord, something to which he had to devote creativity and time.

Are you this clear about your purpose? Do you listen not only for your purpose but for that of others with whom you live and work? And are you being faithful to this divine entrustment?

Lord, I want and need this kind of clarity in my life. I want to be able to describe my purpose so clearly that others can describe it as well. Give me the grace for clarity and then more grace so I may be a faithful steward of this divine entrustment from You. I want to be a person of purpose!

PURPOSE REVIVAL

DIVINE ENERGY

"But on the contrary, seeing that I had been entrusted with the gospel to the uncircumcised, just as Peter had been to the circumcised (for He who effectually worked for Peter in his apostleship to the circumcised effectually worked for me also to the Gentiles). . ." - Galatians 2:7-9.

You'll be successful in your purpose because God works as your partner with and through you. The Greek word for the phrase *effectually worked* is the word from which we get our English word *energy*. You can therefore conclude that when you work in your purpose, you have divine energy, which you can see when you study both Peter's and Paul's lives. They achieved more than seemed humanly possible because a divine energy flowed through them in their purpose.

JOHN W. STANKO   87

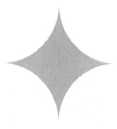

Where do you have divine energy? What can you do that, although you may get fatigued, you always bounce back with enthusiasm and creativity? If you don't have this kind of energy, what kind of changes do you need to make to get and keep it?

Lord, I want to work with divine energy and that means I must work in the purpose You assigned me. I don't want only to be energetic, I also want to be effectively energetic for You. Help me recognize my purpose by the energy I have for a task and then help me harness that energy for Your work and glory.

PURPOSE REVIVAL

JANUARY 14

DAY
45

SHORT AND SWEET

"This is he who was spoken of through the prophet Isaiah: 'A voice of one calling in the wilderness, 'Prepare the way for the Lord, make straight paths for him'"
- Matthew 3:3.

This is the purpose summary for John the Baptist. Notice how short and concise it was: *prepare the way for the Lord*. It's also important to know that it was a biblical phrase taken from the book of Isaiah.

Your purpose statement should be as short and sweet as that. What's more, you'll probably have a Bible verse or passage to go with your statement that enhances and enriches your purpose definition.

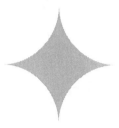

What's your purpose summary? Do you have a Bible passage to go with it? If not, don't fret, but use today's lesson to focus your search so you'll know what you're looking for, and what it will look like when you find it.

Lord, I crave this kind of simplicity and clarity of purpose for my life. Help me see it and also give me a biblical context for it so I may be rooted and grounded in Your will. I know You want me to do Your will, so I thank You in advance for what You'll ultimately reveal to me.

WHAT COMES TO YOU?

*"This is he who was spoken of
through the prophet Isaiah: 'A voice
of one calling in the wilderness,
'Prepare the way for the Lord, make
straight paths for him'"*
- Matthew 3:3.

Yesterday we saw this purpose statement for John the Baptist. When you think of it, John never had to go looking for purpose; it came looking for him. He went to a remote area to baptize, had a strange outfit and unusual diet, and preached a demanding message. Yet all of Israel came to see him, even those who didn't acknowledge or accept his mission.

The same will be true for you. All you have to do is recognize and clarify your purpose, and God will bring the purpose opportunities to you.

What situation, need, or type of people always seem to come to you? What does that say about your purpose? How can you make yourself easier to be found by those who need your purpose expression?

Lord, open my eyes to see the purpose that has been pursuing me my entire life. I don't want to look past the obvious. I trust that You want me not only to find purpose, but also to fulfill it, so You'll bring the opportunities to me. All I have to do is obey and go with the flow. I thank You for making it that simple!

PURPOSE REVIVAL

BEFORE BIRTH

*"Before I formed you in the womb
I knew you, before you were born I
set you apart; I appointed you as a
prophet to the nations"*
- Jeremiah 1:5.

The Lord told Jeremiah that He had assigned him the purpose of a prophet to the nations prior to Jeremiah's birth. The same is true for you, for the Lord assigns your purpose before you are born. It's clear, simple, and doesn't change.

How you express your purpose will probably change, but the essence of who you are and what you do best will not. What's more, you'll often gravitate toward your purpose early in life, and prior to having a relationship with the Lord.

Do you have this kind of simplicity and clarity of purpose? What are you doing to get

that kind of understanding? What price are you willing to pay to get it?

Lord, You want me to know and fulfill my purpose. I ask you to show me who I am and what I was created to do. Send me people who will help me see and then help me understand how to do it with grace and effectiveness. Help me see how childhood experiences may hold clues to my purpose.

ANOINTED

". . . how God anointed Jesus of Nazareth with the Holy Spirit and power, and how he went around doing good and healing all who were under the power of the devil, because God was with him" - Acts 10:38.

It may be difficult for you to consider yourself anointed, for that seems like a church word used when someone preaches or teaches. Yet you accomplish your purpose the same way Jesus did His, and that's by the anointing or power of the Spirit—no matter how simple or mundane your purpose may be.

You're to go and do good through that purpose anointing, however the good is defined for you. Another way of describing this anointing is that God is with you when you perform your purposeful deeds.

When do you sense God's presence with you? What are you doing when He's with you? How can you do those things more often and more effectively than you are now?

Lord, when I flow in purpose, it's only because You're with me and that enables and empowers me. Now show me where I'm to 'go' so I may do good deeds and help others just like Jesus did. I'll no longer resist this anointing, but will take Your presence with me in the power of my purpose as often as possible.

PURPOSE REVIVAL

DAY 49

LOOKING FOR YOU

JANUARY 18

"When a Samaritan woman came to draw water, Jesus said to her, 'Will you give me a drink?'" - John 4:7.

Jesus never had to go looking for purpose opportunities; they always came looking for Him. In John 4, He was sitting by a well resting when a needy woman came to draw water at an unusual time of day for that work (she probably chose the hour to avoid the other women due to her sordid life). Jesus engaged her in conversation and before the day was done, a revival had broken out in that village.

It's the same with your purpose; it comes looking for you, and you can be so accustomed to it that you may not recognize it as anything special.

What situation or problem always seems to find you, no matter where you are or how many are with you? What kind of people do you always seem to encounter and where are they when you do? What do you always seem to have that they need?

Lord, I understand I can be looking for purpose everywhere except where I should, and that is the history and daily activity in my own life! Show me where I'm looking past my purpose because I don't think what I do and who I am are particularly interesting or important. Help me see me for who I truly am.

HEMMING AND HAWING

"Even in the case of lifeless things that make sounds, such as the pipe or harp, how will anyone know what tune is being played unless there is a distinction in the notes? Again, if the trumpet does not sound a clear call, who will get ready for battle?"
- 1 Corinthians 14:7-8.

Purpose can be made more difficult to find because you've been conditioned not to talk about yourself. Therefore, you may be hemming and hawing when you're asked to describe it, using terms like *maybe, I think, sort of,* and *kind of,* being careful not to draw attention to yourself or to seem like you are bragging.

Today's passage indicates you need to make a clear sound about who you are for it's to make a difference in the lives of other people. There's a big

difference in "I think my purpose may be, sort of, you know, to bring joy where there's despair" and "My purpose is to bring joy where there's despair."

Do you struggle when you have to talk about yourself? Do you frame your purpose with tentative or bold words? Are you afraid of this kind of clarity because then you're accountable for producing results according to who you are?

Lord, I've thought it was wrong to draw attention to myself by making a clear, strong statement of purpose, but no longer. I want to have a clear, bold summary of who You have made me to be that I'll then be able to share it with anyone who will listen, knowing that ultimately the main beneficiary of that clarity is me.

PURPOSE REVIVAL

HUMDRUM

*"God blessed them and said to them,
'Be fruitful and increase in number;
fill the earth and subdue it. Rule over
the fish in the sea and the birds in the
sky and over every living creature
that moves on the ground'"*
- Genesis 1:28.

Notice that God blessed Adam by giving him a statement of purpose. Your purpose isn't drudgery or busy work. It's a *blessing* from God that brings you joy and significance, that God then uses to bless others. What's more, it's your sphere in which you bear fruit that glorifies God.

Have you received your purpose assignment and blessing? Are you bearing fruit or settling for being a nice person? Is your life one of humdrum work or exhilarating assignments?

*Lord, I want the blessing of purpose. I want the
kind of clarity that will release me into joyful
work and ministry for You, work that will bear
abundant fruit that glorifies You and helps others.
I refuse to settle for humdrum work but want
Your best for me and others, which comes from
my joyful engagement in a specific purpose.*

PURPOSE REVIVAL

INDISPENSABLE TEAM

"The Lord God said, 'It is not good for the man to be alone. I will make a helper suitable for him'" - Genesis 2:18.

It isn't good for you to be alone in your life, work, or ministry for many reasons. One of those reasons is your God-imposed limitations. God limited your purpose and gifts so you would learn to rely on other people in their purpose to do what you can't do in yours. This requires that you know your purpose and gifts as well as those of others, and that you learn to work together.

Are you familiar and comfortable with your own strengths and limitations? Do you try to do and be it all, or have you learned to rely on others? Who are your indispensable teammates who complement who you are and what you do?

Lord, I don't always like to rely on others, but I know I need them to fill in the gaps created by my limitations. This is Your idea, for You are glorified when teams walk and work together. Open my eyes to this need and show me my teammates; then give us grace to function as one.

PURPOSE REVIVAL

DOORS

*". . . because a great door for effective
work has opened to me, and there are
many who oppose me"*
- 1 Corinthians 16:9.

God wants you to fulfill your purpose more than you do. Therefore, He opens great doors for effective service in the area of your purpose, just like He did for Paul. When a door opens, it's important that you do your part and walk through the door for you don't know how long it will remain open.

That also means when the door closes, you shouldn't try to break it down, but rather move on to the next open door—that process is called change.

Where is there an open door for you right now? Are you ignoring it, hoping that another

more convenient door will open to you? Are you banging on doors that are closed or no longer open?

Lord, I sometimes linger when doors open and persist when they close. I need to be more flexible and open to change as I respond to open doors, and I also need to graciously and quickly respond when they close. Help me recognize the open doors in my life so I can walk, even run, through them to discover the effectiveness that awaits me on the other side.

ENEMIES

". . . because a great door for effective work has opened to me, and there are many who oppose me"
- 1 Corinthians 16:9.

Your opponents in life often don't show up until you start to function and flow in purpose. Joseph, David, Daniel, Paul, and Jesus didn't have any enemies until they started their public purpose, and then people lined up to oppose and even hate them!

If those great purpose heroes had opposition, then you will, too! In fact, your opponents confirm that you're doing something right and don't indicate that you've missed the Lord or stepped out on your own without His protection.

Who's working against your purpose work? Have you allowed them to unnerve you

by their criticism? Can you see they're simply indicating you're on the right path?

*Lord, I don't always deal well with opposition,
but I see today it's part of my purpose territory.
Therefore, I pray for my critics. I'll also make more
of an effort to listen to my critics to see what
I can learn, but I won't give in to my critics by
shrinking back in fear or limiting how I carry out
my purpose work.*

PURPOSE REVIVAL

ANOINTING

"You have loved righteousness and hated wickedness; therefore God, your God, has set you above your companions by anointing you with the oil of joy" - Hebrews 1:9.

The leading indicator that confirms you're functioning in your purpose is joy. God gives you joy in what He wants You to do and be, so you'll know His will in any given moment. It doesn't make sense that God would create you to enjoy something and then not let you do it!

From today's verse, you can see that this joy is part of your anointing, for it brings with it the ability to perform beyond your natural capabilities.

Where in life is your greatest joy? Do you see it as an anointing that empowers you

to work with effectiveness and great energy, thus garnering results for God's glory? Are you fighting or ignoring this joy?

Lord, there are times I've felt this anointing of joy, but haven't always known what to do with it. Today, I understand not to fight it but to surrender to it, for by doing so, I'm embracing my purpose. I thank You for making plain to me what I'm to do, and I vow to make the most of the opportunities You give me.

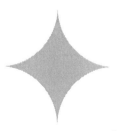

COP OUT

"I can do all this through him who gives me strength" - *Philippians 4:13.*

This oft-quoted verse is a favorite verse for many people, but can actually be used as a cop-out to escape responsibility for bearing fruit. Just because you *can* do something doesn't mean you *will* do it. It just means you have the capability or the potential to do it.

So if you can do all things in Christ, then it begs the questions: **"What are you doing?"** What **acts or deeds are you performing right now with supernatural strength from God? What obstacles are you overcoming as you pursue your goals, flow creatively, and fulfill purpose?**

What more can you be doing in the strength that God provides? In other words, you must put yourself into situations where you trust

that this strength will sustain you. However, that strength may not show up until you need it and not before.

Lord, I don't want to use Your Word to escape my responsibilities and possibilities, but rather employ it to help me accept and fulfill them. I've quoted this verse many times, and now I see that it should be my motto and not my escape. Show me where I can do more and I'll rely on this truth to see me through.

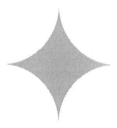

PURPOSE REVIVAL

STRENGTH

"I can do all this through him who gives me strength" - Philippians 4:13.

Purpose is essential because it releases God's strength in your life. This is so because your purpose is doing what you love and brings you joy, and Nehemiah told the people, "the joy of the Lord is your strength" (Nehemiah 8:10).

Therefore, this verse doesn't mean you can do anything within the universe of possibilities, but rather you can do anything that God created you to do with supernatural strength.

Are you operating in that supernatural strength on a daily basis? Is joy the fuel in your purpose tank that allows you to drive fast and far? Is the joy flowing in your life or are you cut off from that which would release the power of your potential?

Lord, I desperately want (and need) the strength only You can provide, but I know it can't come unless I'm doing Your will in Your way. One way to know that I'm in Your will is to follow the joy in my heart and not try to figure it out. Instead, I'll flow in joy and let the joy lead and strengthen me.

PURPOSE REVIVAL

YOUR VERSE

"He went to Nazareth, where he had been brought up, and on the Sabbath day he went into the synagogue, as was his custom. He stood up to read, and the scroll of the prophet Isaiah was handed to him. Unrolling it, he found the place where it is written: 'The Spirit of the Lord is on me, because he has anointed me to proclaim good news to the poor. He has sent me to proclaim freedom for the prisoners and recovery of sight for the blind, to set the oppressed free, to proclaim the year of the Lord's favor'" - Luke 4:16-19.

Jesus had a passage of Scripture that defined His purpose and mission. You may say "Well, that was Jesus," but in all probability, you have one

too. This verse or passage describes who you are and what you were created to do and, once you find it, it can help serve to guide your life decisions and time management.

Have you identified a passage that defines who you are? If you haven't found it yet, then can you list some of your favorite verses to see what if anything they have in common that hold clues to your purpose? Are you fulfilling what your passage identifies as your purpose?

Lord, I want my purpose to be grounded in and directed by Your word. Open my eyes to see where my passage is, and then more importantly give me the power to be and do what it describes. I want to be faithful to what the Spirit of the Lord is upon me to do!

NICKNAME

"Joseph, a Levite from Cyprus, whom the apostles called Barnabas (which means 'son of encouragement')"
- Acts 4:36.

Most don't know Barnabas' real name, which was Joseph. Instead, they know him by his nickname, the one the apostles gave him and, of course, that name has stuck for all time. He didn't get this particular nickname by encouraging every once in a while. He got it because he was consumed with his purpose, which was to encourage anyone within earshot. That's how your purpose should be—not a hobby or part-time activity, but an all-consuming passion that others notice.

What's your all-consuming passion? What would people nickname you in response to what they see you purposefully doing?

Lord, I thank You for Barnabas' example of being totally devoted to his purpose. That's the kind of life I want to live as well. Help me to move beyond dabbling in purpose and allow me to be so clear and focused that others will recognize and know my purpose as well.

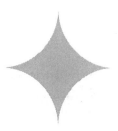

THE ESSENCE

". . . [Barnabas] sold a field he owned and brought the money and put it at the apostles' feet" - Acts 4:37.

Barnabas was the son of encouragement, and everything he did seemed to encourage others—that's how he got his nickname. In this verse, we learn that he gave away the proceeds from the sale of a field he owned for the good of others.

You may be involved in many activities but those aren't your purpose; they're how you express your purpose, which is the essence of who you are, the main effect produced from what you do. In his giving, Barnabas encouraged, because that was the effect he was created to have no matter what he was doing.

Are you distinguishing between what you do and the essence of who you are? What

is the main effect produced from what you do: joy, peace, order, strength? Can you see that effect as being part or all of your purpose?

Lord, I can do many things but I want to know my purpose in all those things. Make my purpose clear through all those things so I can know who I am and be true to that as often as possible. Help me distinguish between what I do and who I am!

PURPOSE REVIVAL

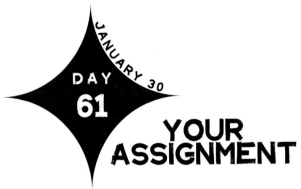

YOUR ASSIGNMENT

"I [Jesus] have brought you glory on earth by finishing the work you gave me to do" - John 17:4.

Jesus brought glory to the Father by finishing the work He was assigned to do. In other words, He glorified God by fulfilling His purpose. Paul said the same thing except he termed it running the race.

You won't glorify God by singing, preaching, or holiness, but by righteous acts of purpose that only you can do because they're God's assignment for you to do them.

How will you bring God glory in this lifetime? What is it that's uniquely yours to do? How will you know when you have finished that work?

Lord, I want to bring You glory and I see today that I'll do so by and through my life of purpose. I have a work to do that no one else can perform like I can, so I need to be busy doing that. Help me focus on my assignment and produce the work that will glorify Your name before men.

PURPOSE REVIVAL

YOUR CHOICE

*"But the Pharisees and the experts
in the law rejected God's purpose for
themselves, because they had not
been baptized by John"* - Luke 7:30.

You have a choice where purpose is concerned. You can choose never to search and find it or you can find it and for whatever reason reject it. At that point, our sovereign God will choose someone else to fulfill the plans He had for you. That doesn't mean He doesn't love you, but the loss is all yours as you forfeit the joys and exhilaration of being used by God for something special.

What's your attitude toward your purpose? Are you excited or indifferent? Passive or aggressive? Are you waiting for or wading into the opportunity?

Lord, I don't want to miss my purposeful life through waiting, fear, or apathy. I choose to accept Your purpose assignment and vow to pursue it with all my heart and strength out of devotion to You. I further commit to prepare myself and seize every opportunity to make a difference for Your glory! Amen.

KEEP IN TOUCH WITH JOHN STANKO

www.purposequest.com
www.johnstanko.us
www.stankobiblestudy.com
www.stankomondaymemo.com

or via email at johnstanko@gmail.com

John also does extensive relief and community development work in Kenya. You can see some of his projects at:

www.purposequest.com/contributions

PurposeQuest International
PO Box 8882
Pittsburgh, PA 15221-0882

TO FIND OTHER PROJECTS BY URBAN PRESS, GO TO:

www.urbanpress.us

to discuss publishing
your own work,
please contact
john stanko at:

johnstanko@purposequest.com